THE HEART'S LANDS

ACKNOWLEDGEMENTS

My thanks go to the Rev. Sally Brown who arranged
and accompanied my trip to New Mexico
and to sculptor Amelie Starkey who lent us Heronway.

Thanks to Susan Garrett and Jane Rotch;
their enthusiasm about my poems gave me courage.

Thanks to the Rev. Cathy Newport for transport service.

Worlds of gratitude to Esther de Waal for her kind preface,
and for the wonderful evening at The Cwm
that gave birth to the book.

Without Michael Woodward, mid-wife, gentle editor
and patient friend, the book would not be.

Most of all, thanks be to the Word.

THE HEART'S LANDS

BONNIE THURSTON

p³p

PS
3570
. H89
H4
2001

Published in Great Britain 2001
THREE PEAKS PRESS
9 Croesonen Road
Abergavenny
Monmouthshire NP7 6AE
mail@p3p.org   http://p3p.org

Designed & set in Joanna at Three Peaks Press

Printed in Wales at Gwasg Dinefwr, Llandybie

A CIP record for this publication
is available from the British Library

ISBN   1—902093—05—4

CONTENTS

PREFACE

IN THIS short volume we see an artist at work with a touch that is both pure and profound. In her hands stones live and become bread to feed our hungers, and holy places transform us. We are given images that are simple and resonant, and then we are given words that cascade:

> a grinning Pan
> smirking fertility
> disgorging vegetation.

Writing of St Kevin with the blackbird's eggs, she says:

> her whole world
> in your hands.

She shows us the voices of the world around us, helping us to become aware of the elements of rock and water, of the landscapes that heal, redeem, sing, or murmur of what was and what might have been. . . . When she tells us that St Brendan journeyed into the unknown to show us the way home the same might also be said of her—except that we are shown the familiar in a way that allows it to become new and strange.

We are led into place: we encounter Celtic saints but finally we meet the poet herself, in her struggles and in her strength, and it is that generosity which above all puts us firmly in her debt.

Esther de Waal

NEW MEXICO POEMS

"The words are all that matter,
you send them out as a prayer,
hoping to become invisible behind them."

Kathleen Norris

Northern New Mexico

I CARRY your landscape
before my inner eye:
blue and pink expansiveness,
stars that stretch on forever.
It has blown out my heart's walls.

Familiar geography
is no longer familiar.
The fences have come down.
Once known landmarks are blurred.

Wild thyme and sage grow
with domesticated mint,
enlarge my heart's garden,
ending its orderly rows.

A great, delicious freedom
unfurls on my horizon
like the gold, mauve and red
ribbons of your sunset.
Even night falls brightly.

It's said that, for God, night
is as bright as the day.
It must be God flung out
across your black expanse,
twinkling in the darkness,
shattering categories.

Mora River
Watrous, New Mexico

A RIVER snakes around the ranches,
nourishes tall, green grass
and wild asparagus,
makes the cactus bloom
and gives the kids a place to play.
Hawks nest in rocks above it.
Small, sly creatures live near its banks.

And there's a lion by the river.
We've seen its silent prints by the path,
a white rib cage rising crazily
from the green fecundity.
In the midst of life we are in death.

It's a lively place by day,
the winding river way,
but don't linger at dusk
when darkness stalks nearby.
Go on home to supper.
Things hungrier than you lurk here.

Coyote

ALL WAS still and there was no moon
but the sky was awash with stars
as I walked through perfumed darkness
headed for the kiva and rest.
Then I heard for the first, sweet time
your wonderful, terrible song.

Exhilarated – and frightened –
I stopped, hearing all loneliness
and outrage of the human heart
focused in one, long, night-piercing
animal note, sostenuto
worthy of tragic opera.

I longed to sing that aria
to howl at the vast expanses,
cry out to the stars to attend.
But I. . . I could not give it voice
constrained as I am by language,
trapped by monotone in my heart.

A wary dog facing danger,
the hair on my neck stood straight up.
And then came the joyful release:
to hear it wordlessly uttered,
all there in one, great, gorgeous cry—
your howling communion enough.

Watrous to Taos

TRAVELLING WITH a holy woman
there are long silences
as the journey winds
through high, green meadows
and run down towns
like the coal camps
I grew up in:
once, but no future.

Drawn to solitary places,
occasionally we emerge
in tentative language.
No good at small talk,
chit-chat annoys me,
but I'm ill at ease
with the space
that hangs between
my fellow pilgrim and me.
Awkwardly, I confess it.

"The conversation," she says,
"is going on all around us."
And so it is—
God populates earth and air,
mute and palpable.

Highway Crosses

THEY'RE ugly, those wooden crosses
festooned with plastic flowers
and bunting and ribbon,
set up at dangerous intersections,
or by careening ravines,
or on curling mountain roads,
or those too tempting straight stretches.

They're death markers,
synthetically bright, colorful momento mori,
warnings, reminders, talismen,
sentinels whose duty it is to watch,
to send ravenous death packing.
Not here, not again.

"Once you had a feast here,
a young, promising santero,
drunken lovers,
a family on the way to Mass.
Well the café is closed.
Go get your chilies somewhere else—
or starve."

Decorated wooden crosses
mark a via dolorosa.
They belong here with the bloody Christs.
They belong here with the weeping Marys.
Oh how sweetly they belong here,
silent, tasteless, touching witnesses of faith.

Santuario Chimayo

SHE CAME to a place
where hurts are healed,
the *abuelita*,
walked straight to the cross,
put down her purse,
lit her candles,
and talked to Jesus
in familiar language.

Wounded, I too had come,
though not so sure as she
that Jesus stretches out
His broken hands to heal.
"Christ, where is your comforting?
Lamb of God so cruelly killed,
Jesus, keep me near the cross,
and one day look on me."

Hollyhocks

THEY'RE exploding
profuse, vibrant
color against
buff adobe.
They stretch upward
toward a sky so blue
even Mary
wouldn't wear it.

Sing out crimson,
pink and white!
Praise with green
in noonday sun!
Shadows lengthen.
Soon enough,
flowers fall
to ashen dust.

Taos Mountain

WE LIFT up our eyes to her
dressed in purpley-green
and crowned with clouds.
She hovers maternally
over her famous town
now full of the flaky
and the faithful, the odd,
the beautiful, the trashy.

She presided over history,
suffered her recalcitrant children,
watched pueblo and hacienda grow,
saw Pope drive out Popé,
absorbed the blood of all
who could not live together,
took to her breast those who came
with cross and sword,
with plow and pen and paintbrush.
She feels deer-dressed Indians
march down her spine
and whispers, "not another Long Walk."

They say an eagle
first led people here
to live under her shadow.
Later, she married
Sangre de Christo,
apt name for this magic mountain,
this spell binding woman,
this place of holiness and resistance.

Dare we draw too near
or touch?

Rio Grande Gorge

It's unexpected
cutting as it does
a long, flat highway.

Suddenly the earth
drops away
and far, far below
is the river
so distant
its roar is silenced.

I walk out on the bridge,
look down seduced.
The dizzying depth
invites light-headedness,
a sense of imbalance.
I embrace wind, water, rock
and the omnipresent sky
wider and higher
than the river is deep.

In the contest of elements
the rock concedes;
water eventually wins,
patiently through the ages
etching its deep
wrinkle in earth's face.

The cut is not a scar
but a reminder:
yield to living water.

Stations of the Cross
San Luis, Colorado

TWENTY MILES from the border,
an ordinary enough town,
save for its faith.

Is it the *koinonia* heritage
of common land and water
that made this place?

Or the *Geist* of the name
Sangre de Christo
that gave this parish power?

Whatever, love built
fifteen stations on the mesa,
adding resurrection
to its modern miracle.

Never say never.
When you believe
you feed on God's body,
slake your thirst in God's blood,
God will come to you mightily
and make you eat the word
and live.

Holy Places: A Prayer for Sally

LIKE POTTERS' vessels,
some landscapes
reform us,
whirl us on their wheels,
bring us from their kilns
glazed and new.

There mountains
grace the horizon
without blocking the view.
There pine trees
gnarled by wind
bend and survive.

Night brings rest;
the moon rises
on silence, safety, sleep.
In the morning
small blue flowers
open among thorns.

Arid places
of dust, stone and heat
become fecund.
The desert blossoms;
streams break forth
to water holy ground.

Open spaces
heal the heart hurts
of our small darkness
into which light shines
with the wideness
of God's mercy.

Some landscapes
redeem us
to paint and sing,
to play in shadow,
dance in wind;
to be green again.

Mission Churches

SQUAT AND square
(enlarged children's blocks)
humbly made
sun-dried clay
into which God
continues to breathe
the breath of life,
the adobe churches
seem natural here.

They are *sipapu*,
calling us in
from bright blue heat
to a cool gloom
where living and dead,
saints, *santos* and sinners
are gathered together
under *vigas* as rough and loving
as the arms of Christ's cross.

And we enter:
the tourist to gape;
the pious to pray.
Latinos and Indians,
the white and the brown,
we blink in darkness,
wait for our eyes to adjust
and hope to see
what we came for.

These vast expanses
this wild, perilous country
grew a solid church
with wider doors
than their founders envisioned,
wide as Christ's arms on the cross.

CELTIC CULDEES

"After the silent centuries I weave their praise.
The core of faith is one and it is splendid to know
Souls that are one with the quick in the root of Being."
from *Dail Pren*, Waldo Williams

I praise these martyrs,
red, white or green.
I praise these martyrs,
and the God they've seen.

I. ST. PATRICK

WHAT shall we say of Patrick
the quintessential Irishman
who wasn't?

Son of a British deacon
who was son of a priest,
you were stolen by pirates,
enslaved in Ireland.
For six long years
you tended sheep,
then went home
on the strength of a dream.

You trained in Gaul,
took up the family business,
then the Dream-Maker
called you back
to bitter Ireland
to pastor His flock,
to teach His people,
to be an icon of forgiveness.

Dare we believe the stories
of serpents and shamrocks,
of Druids silenced at Tara?
Dare we believe your prayer
that God the Three-in-One,
the strength of all dreamers,
is before and behind,
above, below and with us?

Patrick, be our breastplate,
stand between us
and the darkness.

II. BRIGID OF KILDARE

BRIGID shares her fertile feast
with a Druid goddess.
She, like the church
in her land,
is wedded to something
older than Christ.

Mary of the Gael
called women to Kildare
to community,
a city of the poor,
with fire at its heart,
fire not to be put out.

When he raised his hand
to bless her nun's vows,
the Bishop Mel saw
tongues of fire on her head,
fire which took his tongue,
for he spoke her bishop.

Brigid of untameable goodness,
who sold the sword for the poor,
who drove the devil back
with a cross of straw,
Brigid, who wears a mitre of fire,
may your tribe increase.

III. ILLTUD

ILLTUD, son of Cassian's house,
made his own in Wales
a center for study,
a home for art.

Llanilltyd grew
and consumed its land.
So Illtud took his staff,
drew a line in the sand
and forbade the sea to cross.

Illtud, whom the sea obeyed,
withdrew to a lonely place to pray,
and crossed the sea to Brittany,
a pilgrim known
for all he knew.

Most learned
of all the Britons,
teach us, Illtud,
where to draw the line.

IV. ITA OF KILLEEDY

MOTHER Ita,
your nuns at Limerick
taught boys like Brendan.
Was it you who made them
so restless for God
that they sailed small ships
to the edge of the sea?
Was the hard life
you chose for yourself,
martyrdom's green way,
meant to slake
that self same thirst
which, being woman,
you could not quench
by voyaging?

V. DAVID OF WALES

DEWI, the saint maker,
patron of Welshmen
(fierce warriors
who sing like angels)
was one of them.

White martyr,
he wandered from Wales,
to the city of God,
in holy Zion
was given his chair,
returned home primate,
built twelve houses
known for their harshness,
gave his name
to fifty places,
and when he preached
the earth itself
rose up beneath his feet
so all could see
and hear the Waterman
tell of the ways of God.

Dewi, saint maker,
make of our soldiers singers.
Our mountains will sing with them,
and all the trees of the forest
will clap their hands.

VI. BRENDAN THE NAVIGATOR

HE founded a house,
but hungered for homelessness.
To arrive was his snare,
to journey, his freedom.

He sought the sea's rootlessness,
peregrinatio por Dei amore,
sailed his curach from Cork
to discover his desert
in pathless waters.

He voyaged
into the unknown
to find the Land of Promise,
to show us the way home.

VII. COLUMBA OF IONA

THE Dove flew
to a place of water,
wind and rock,
a place beyond
sight of home,
out at earth's edge,
out where the sea drops off
into empty air.

The Dove knew
we always stand
facing the end
which makes now
sweet, full
and fragile.

VIII. KENTIGERN OF GLASGOW

FROM inauspicious birth
you became Glasgow's
most dear shepherd,
then a white martyr.

Exiled from your chair,
beloved of the Dove,
patron of the fallen,
soul-son of Magdalene
who loved much,
guide us gently
with your staff.
Prod us lest we fall.

IX. KEVIN

MONKS taught you,
but you did not dwell
with your brothers,
went the hermit's way,
prayed alone.

A blackbird
laid her eggs
in your hand.
You held them
until they hatched,
her whole world
in your hands.

The heavens are God's;
the earth God gives us.
Teach us to love this world,
to hold its eggs gently;
and when they hatch
to open our hands
and glory in flight.

X. AIDAN OF LINDISFARNE

LIKE as the hart
longeth for the water,
you with your twelve
fled like a stag
from the home of the Dove
to an isle in the sea
and made of its rock
a cradle of Christianity.

Your house put its wealth
at the feet of the poor.
Your isle is called holy;
it gave up its store.

XI. HILDA OF WHITBY

OF noble birth,
christened by a saint,
she became a nun,
abbess of a double house.
She wrote its rule,
insisted scripture be studied,
mothered arts and learning,
nurtured Caedmon
who first hymned
heaven-kingdom's Guardian
in our native tongue.

In 664
she opened her door
because she knew
the rune of hospitality.
She kept it to the letter,
and it spelled the doom
of her way of life.

XII. CUTHBERT

HE began tending sheep,
in a vision of light
saw the angels carrying
souls to heaven.

Melrose made
the shepherd a monk,
and the monk, a pastor,
an itinerant servant of souls.

Lindisfarne made
the pastor a prior
whose heart longed
for an anchor-hold.

He found it at Farne.
But the Church
called the hermit
to shepherd its souls,

and when the bishop died
moved his obedient bones
from the Holy Isle
to the cathedral he'd fled.

Poor, strong Cuthbert
gave so much
and got so little,
not even a quiet tomb.

THE CELTIC CULDEES

IT wasn't Rome
brought their demise
(though prelates
tell the tale thus),
but Viking raiders
killed and took
them captive,
carried away
what little they had.

These dear martyrs,
companions of God,
are not gone
who faithfully left
illuminated maps
of the heart's lands,
stone churches,
high crosses,
the call of anchor-hold,
the lure of pilgrimage,
the challenge to see,
if only in a mirror darkly,
creation charged
with the glory of heaven,
and God's hand
guiding our curach
to the harbor home
of heaven's host.

HEREFORDSHIRE
POEMS

Along the Wye

ON A glorious summer day
this border country rolls out
in a carpet of green turf,
the fertile result
of a blood-soaked history.
A place where armies marched,
kings were made and broken;
it was not peaceful
as it seems now.

Cistercians nestled their abbeys
among these verdant hills,
built their common life
around a prayer-soaked emptiness,
the cloisters at their heart.
Now, though they point east
from darkness to light,
in their skeletal remains
only the wind chants the hours.

Border lands often murmur
of what was and might have been.
Like the Welsh it leads to,
this landscape sings.
God draws back the veil
to make a Golden Valley
between the Black Mountains,
a place teeming with the life
of presence and past.

The Church of St Mary and St David, Kilpeck

REMOTE, BEAUTIFULLY proportioned,
made of local red stone,
it stands as it did
in the twelfth century:
solid, rooted, prayerful.

Wondrously decorated with
a green man, Sheela-na-gig,
creatures of a whimsical imagination
that wisely invited
the humorous and hideous to church.

Supported by snakes and vines,
a heavy Norman doorway
summons the pilgrim,
"rekindle hope
all ye who enter here."

Inside, the eye is drawn by arches
through nave to choir
to where, above the altar,
David plays his harp
in a small, colored window.

It is a church for poets
who let the lovely and the lewd,
the beastly and the beautiful,
the pagan and the pious
sit down together.

It is a church for dreamers
and those who know God
delights to dwell
in juxtapositions, silence
and stones that cry out.

It is a church for those
with eyes baptized
in the belly of a font
that stands with its feet
on the Rock of Ages.

Sheela-na-gig on Kilpeck Church

SQUATTING UNDER the eaves,
lewdly grinning down at us,
exposing yourself to all comers,
who brought you to church?
What raucous imagination
dared make you
an ecclesiastical decoration?

One which loved fleshly life,
knew sex is hilarious
and procreation normal;
one which explored
a woman's body and found
treasures in darkness
and riches in secret places.

Green Man

I NEVER met a Green Man
until I stumbled upon him
in Welsh border country.
Then I found him
in every church:
a leafy mask,
a grinning Pan
smirking fertility
in a dusty corner;
or a male head
looking slightly surprised
disgorging vegetation
down a pillar,
over a door frame;
or the hint of a face
furtive behind leaves,
Adam hiding among the trees.

Old as God's third day
and every bit as good,
you flourished
long before the church
grafted you in.
Now, though we try
to tame you, name you
in guide books
and art history,
you burst forth
make even stone live,
turn it to bread
that feeds my hunger
for irrepressible reality.
Root it deep within us,
this healing wholeness,
this wild profusion of life.

Abbey Dore, Ascensiontide

No LONGER lord of the lands
or center of chant and commerce,
a shadow of your former self,
your crossing was salvaged
for a parish church.
The Cistercians were domesticated,
brought down to lay level,
mortified for mortals.

Suddenly, without warning,
singing an Ascension hymn
at an ordinary evensong,
your transfiguration
transforms us.
Lifted up by your coming down,
we need not gaze at heaven
having glimpsed it here.
Feet firmly on good earth,
our voice bears witness to joy

which is always in short supply,
which always enlivens what is dead.
Cloistered spirits
of long departed monks
rise up and attend our song.
Even the martial cries
of your malign neighbors
are stilled by the power of praise.
We sing in your nave.
You rise from your grave.

Norman Churches, Herefordshire

ESCAPING TURBULENT Oxford
I used to bike to Iffley,
sit in the shadows
of that Norman church
and breathe easier.
I did not know
what drew me,
only that it soothed,
calmed, centered.

Thirty years later
I glimpsed the why
here, in these churches
built of local stone,
churches that seem
to rise from earth
without human help
as naturally as hedgerows
and as full of life.

Their square simplicity
is softened
by arch and apse.
No ornate fan vaulting
draws the eye upward.
Homey dog-toothed arches
tie walls firmly to floor,
make the place solid,
embracing, permanent.

Unpretentious churches
house a practical
life of spirit.
No lace cuffs ever offered
or incense accompanied
the coarse broken bread,
the pewter cup
of rough wine
that tastes of earth.

Unpretentious churches
root the life of this land
in the practice of prayer,
at many crossroads
quietly offer all comers
an invitation to pause,
to rest, to remember
that peace passes
understanding.

RETURNING
AND REST

For thus said the Lord God, the Holy One of Israel:
In returning and rest you shall be saved;
in quietness and in trust shall be your strength.

Isaiah 30: 15

1

A random strain of music,
a forgotten melody,
unearths long buried sadness.
Unbidden tears
spring to my eyes,
well over, water
and liberate seeds
hidden, but waiting
in the fallow soil
of my furrowed heart,
now tilled and turned.

2

FINALLY I am returning
to the place almost lost,
back by a circuitous route,
through monotone, monochrome
deserts of rationality:
"there be dragons."

I nearly died of thirst,
but I am going back
to well springs
of color, music, passion,
back to my body,
my own, green home.

I am going home,
and on the road ahead
one is waiting and watching,
softly and tenderly welcoming
with outstretched arms,
"ye who are weary, come home."

3

O Lord,
You are the home
of all my loneliness.
Kindle a fire
in my cold hearth.
Light a candle
in the window
of my darkness.
Call me home to supper.
Crumbs from your table
feed my hungers.
Advent in me;
that in my loving
I may give You away,
and find You again
when night closes
solitary day.

4

THE yoke of human love
weighs down my shoulders,
distributes my load,
keeps me from a private path,
and prevents the suffering
of a solitary way.
It ties me to earth,
teaches me heaven.
It fills me with fear,
and dares me to hope.
Oh love of the Beloved,
are you burden
or are you joy?

5

INSCRUTABILITY
is not inviting:
a door without handles,
the darkened cellar,
vast expansive heavens,
mental conundrums.

God, beyond our knowing,
Being so silent,
being so vast and far,
loving You is hard.

If just for a moment,
beckon and reveal.
Sing us a quiet song;
bring us bread and wine;
invite us to table
and come, sup with us.

LIFE has seasons
so weary, worn and sad
that the only hand
to reach for
is one love-scarred,
the only comfort
to recline on the bosom
of Him Who knew none,
to drink from His cup,
to welcome
His wounding touch
and being so smitten
(O Lord, I am not worthy)
healed.

7

I lay my weary head
on God's immense shoulder
and find myself held
in loving embrace.
Bitter fruit has ripened
to an intense sweetness—
though even yet
may need be crushed,
matured to wine.
But now, here,
loving and loved,
it is enough
to rest, to yield,
to wait.

8

WE have lived stormily together,
but now You draw me
into the eye, to calm
amid changes and chances.
I repose here
in quiet consolation.

Constant God
of weather and seasons,
in storm make me
a peaceful place
where others are stilled
and leave blessed.

9

AFTER the rain
and night's deep darkness,
it is still,
and the sun pours in
thick and clear as honey.

It is You, O God,
filling my house
with clarity and Presence,
with that Life
which is Light.

You alone surround me
with bright silence,
embrace me, fill me
with Your infinite sweetness.
You alone are enough.

OTHER TITLES AVAILABLE FROM THREE PEAKS PRESS:

THAT MYSTERIOUS MAN:
ESSAYS ON AUGUSTINE BAKER, 1575-1641
EDITED BY MICHAEL WOODWARD, INTRODUCED BY ROWAN WILLIAMS
ISBN   1-902093-03-8

THOMAS MERTON: POET, MONK, PROPHET
EDITED BY PAUL PEARSON, DANNY SULLIVAN & IAN THOMSON
ISBN   1-902093-01-1

BERNARD WALKE: A GOOD MAN WHO COULD NEVER BE DULL
DONALD ALLCHIN
ISBN   1-902093-02-X

THIRST
MICHAEL WOODWARD
ISBN   1-902093-04-6

MADE AND PRINTED IN WALES BY
GWASG DINEFWR PRESS
LLANDYBIE FOR
THREE PEAKS PRESS
9 CROESONEN ROAD, ABERGAVENNY,
MONMOUTHSHIRE NP7 6AE